BASIC DESIGN OF 400/220KV SUB-STATION

(ELECTRICAL ENGINEERING)

BY

KAMAL KRISHNA MAITY

BASIC DESIGN OF 400/220KV SUB-STATION

The author has had a long association with the Design and Engineering described in this book. The book is the result of this experience and the overwhelming help and support extended to him by colleagues, friends. The purpose of this book is to share the experience of the author with those in the field. It is an attempt to make these subjects simple and interesting. The book should provide an easy approach to answer the problems an engineer or engineering student may face when handling these Design & Engineering. The author is sure that the readers will find ample opportunity to learn from his experience and apply this information to their field of activities. The book aims to provide a bridge between the concept and the application with this book by his or her side, an engineer should be able to apply better, design better and select better equipment for system needs and ambient conditions. It should prove to be a handy reference to all those in the field of design and application, protection and testing, production, project engineering, project implementation or maintenance, in addition to the sales and purchase of these products. Engineers have done an incredible job by inventing new technologies and bringing them, over the years to their present level. Research and development work by a dedicated few scientists and engineers has been an untiring process which has provided us with yet more advanced forms of technology. The credit for this book goes to these engineers throughout the world. The author is not an inventor, nor has he done anything new in these fields. He has only attempted to bring together such advances in a particular field in one book for their better application. The author's contribution can be regarded as an appropriate selection and application of the available technology and products for their optimum utilization. All relevant aspects of a design have been discussed but greater emphasis is laid on selection and application. Since this is a reference book the basic theory is assumed to be known to a student or a practicing engineer handling such machines and/or technologies. In the academic world the derivation of a formula from fundamentals is regarded as most important. In practice, this formula matters more rather than its origin. But for those who wish to know more of the reasoning and the background, care is taken that such subjects are also covered. The author hopes that readers will be satisfied to have most of their queries answered. The book has been written so that it should refresh and awaken the engineer within a reader. The author is certain that this is what readers will feel as they progress through this book. A cursory reading will bring them abreast of the subject and enable them to tackle problems with ease and simplicity. The author's efforts will be defeated if this book falls short of this aim. The endeavor has been to provide as much information as possible on the application of available technology and products. It should help application engineers to select and design a more suitable machine or power system for their needs. As mentioned above, this text will not cover the full engineering derivations, yet all fundamentals have been provided that are considered relevant to engineer any machine or system covered in this book. To augment the information, 'further reading' has also been provided to support the text and to answer queries that may arise on a particular subject. For detailed engineering, the manufacturers are still the best guide In this book, the author has tried to make the subject comprehensive yet concise and easy to understand so that, one can easily refer to it at any time. The references drawn are brief, but pertinent, and adequate to satisfy a query. This book may prove to be a boon to young engineers entering the field. With it they can compare the theory of their studies with application in the field. Whereas all aspects that were thought necessary have been considered, it is possible that some have been omitted. The author would be grateful to receive suggestions from readers for any additions, deletions or omissions to make this book even more useful and up to date.

The electric power substation, whether generating station or transmission and distribution, remains one of the most challenging and exciting fields of electric power engineering. The objective of this book is to provide an extensive overview of the Electrical Engineering as well as a reference and guide for its study. The chapters are written for the electric power engineering professional to give detailed design information, as well as for other engineering professions who want an overview or specific information in one particular area.

Contents

1. IMPORTANT CONSIDERATIONS IN SUBSTATION DESIGN

- Safety of personnel and equipment
- Reliability and Security
- Adherence to
  - Statutory obligations
    - I.E. rules, Environmental aspects
  - Electrical design considerations
  - Structural design considerations
- Ease of maintenance
- Possibility to Expand

2. SYSTEM PARAMETERS

Sr.	Description	400kV	220kV	
1.	Nominal system voltage	400kV	220kV	
2.	Max. operating voltage	420kV	245kV	
3.	Rated frequency	50Hz	50Hz	
4.	Number of phases	3	3	
5.	System neutral earthing	Effectively earthed		
6.	Corona Extinction voltage	320kV	156kV	
7.	Min. creepage distance	25mm/kV	25mm/kV	
8.	Rated short ckt. Current for 1 sec.	40kA	40kA	
10.	Radio interference voltage at 1MHZ (for phase to earth voltage)	1000 mV (320kV)	1000 mV (156kV)	

Sr.	Description	400kV	220kV	Remarks
11.	Rated insulation levels i) Full wave impulse withstand voltage -- for lines -- for reactor/ X'mer -- for other equipments	 1550kVp 1300kVp 1425kVp	 1050kVp 950kVp 1050kVp	
	ii) Switching impulse withstand voltage (dry/wet)	1050kVp		
	iii) One min. power freq. withstand voltage (dry/wet) -- for lines -- for CB / Isolator -- for other equipments	 680kV 520kV 610kV 630kV	 460kV 460kV 530kV 460kV	 (Line-ground) (open terminals)

3. SUBSTATION BIRD'S VIEW

4. 400KV CIRCUIT BREAKER

5. 400KV ISOLATOR

6. 400KV CURRENT TRANSFORMER

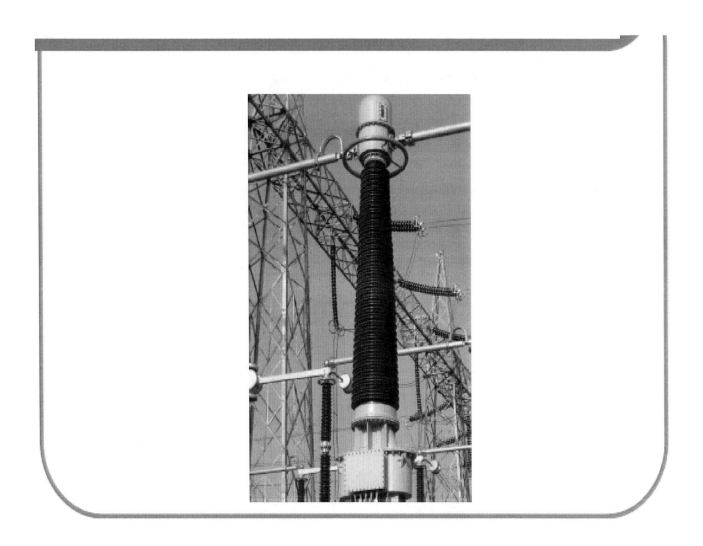

7. 400KV CAPACITIVE VOLTAGE TRANSFORMER (CVT)

8. 400KV SURGE ARRESTER (SA)

9. 400KV SHUNT REACTOR & NGR

10.400/220 KV AUTO TRANSFORMER

11.400KV BUS POST INSULATOR

12.400KV WAVE TRAPS

13. GANTRY

14. FUNCTIONS OF SUBSTATION EQUIPMENTS

Equipment	Function

BASIC DESIGN OF 400/220KV SUB-STATION

1. Bus-Bar	Incoming & outgoing ckts. Connected to bus-bar
2. Circuit Breaker	Automatic switching during normal or abnormal conditions
3. Isolators	Disconnection under no-load condition for safety, isolation and maintenance.
4. Earthing switch	To discharge the voltage on dead lines to earth
5. Current Transformer	To step-down currents for measurement, control & protection
6. Voltage Transformer	To step-down voltages for measurement, control & protection
7. Lightning Arrester	To discharge lightning over voltages and switching over voltages to earth
8. Shunt reactor	To control over voltages by providing reactive power compensation
9. Neutral-Grounding resistor	To limit earth fault current
10. Coupling capacitor	To provide connection between high voltage line & PLCC equipment
11. Line –Trap	To prevent high frequency signals from entering other zones.
12. Shunt capacitors	To provide compensations to reactive loads of lagging power factors
13. Power Transformer	To step-up or step-down the voltage and transfer power from one a.c. voltage another a.c. voltage at the same frequency.
14. Series Capacitor	Compensation of long lines.

15. FUNCTIONS OF ASSOCIATED SYSTEM IN SUBSTATION

System	Function

1. Substation Earthing system
    -- Earthmat
    -- Earthing spikes
    -- Earthing risers
	To provide an earthmat for connecting neural points, equipment body, support structures to earth. For safety of personnel and for enabling earth fault protection. To provide the path for discharging the earth currents from neutrals, faults, Surge Arresters, overheads shielding wires etc. with safe step-potential and touch potential.

2. Overhead earth wire shielding or Lightning masts.	To protect the outdoor substation equipment from lightning strokes.

3. Illumination system (lighting)
    -- for switchyard
    -- buildings
    -- roads etc.	

4. Protection system
    -- protection relay panels
    -- control cables
    -- circuit breakers
    -- CTs, VTs etc.
	To provide alarm or automatic tripping of faulty part from healthy part and also to minimize damage to faulty equipment and associated system.

5. Control cable	For Protective circuits, control circuits, metering circuits, communication circuits
6. Power cable	To provide supply path to various auxiliary equipment and machines.

7. PLCC system power line carries communication system
  -- line trap
  -- coupling capacitor
  -- PLCC panels
	For communication, telemetry, tele-control, power line carrier protection etc.

8. Fire Fighting system
  -- Sensors, detection system
  -- water spray system
  -- fire prot. panels, alarm system
  -- watertank and spray system
	To sense the occurrence of fire by sensors and to initiate water spray, to disconnect power supply to affected region to pin-point location of fire by indication in control room.

9. Auxiliary standby power system
  -- diesel generator sets
  -- switchgear
  -- distribution system
	For supplying starting power, standby power for auxiliaries

10. Telephone, telex, microwave, OPF	For internal and external communication

16. Basic Drawings for Design/Construction

BASIC DESIGN OF 400/220KV SUB-STATION

- Single Line Diagram
- General Arrangement Drawing
- Electrical Plan and Section
- Control Room Architectural layout

- Structural layout
- Earthmat layout
- Civil layout
- Erection Key Diagram
- Lighting Layout

17. SINGLE LINE DIAGRAM – 220KV

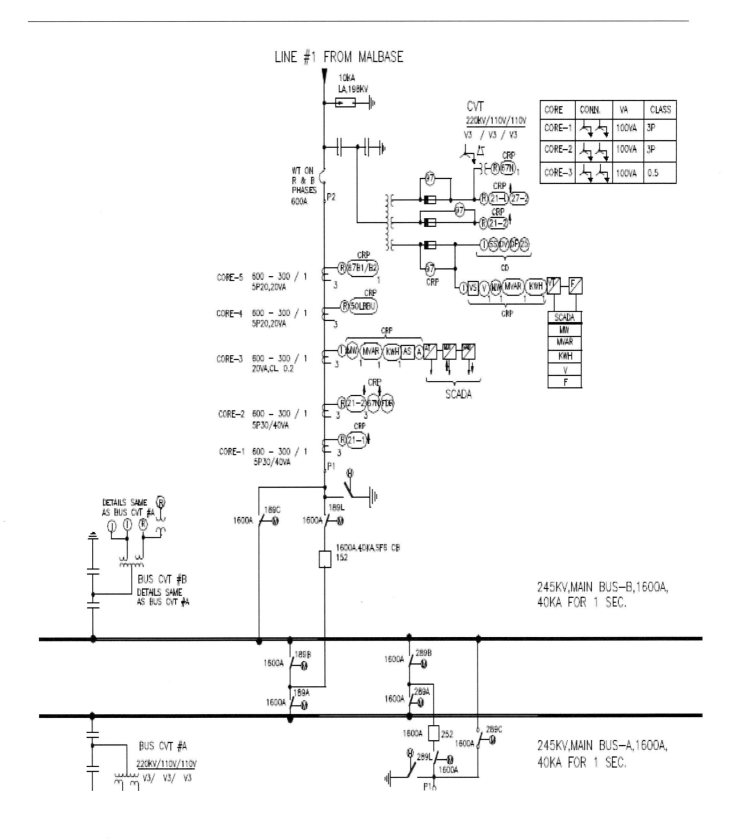

18. SUBSTATION GENERAL ARRANGEMENT LAYOUT

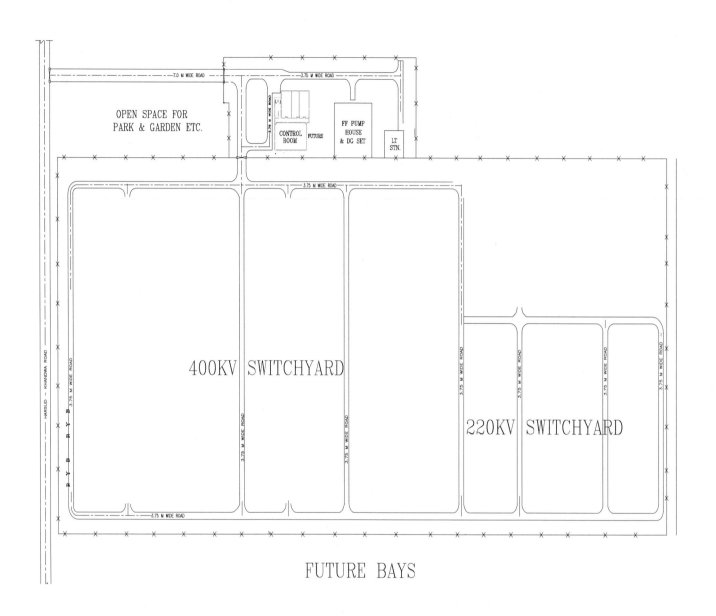

FUTURE BAYS

19. CONTROL ROOM LAYOUT

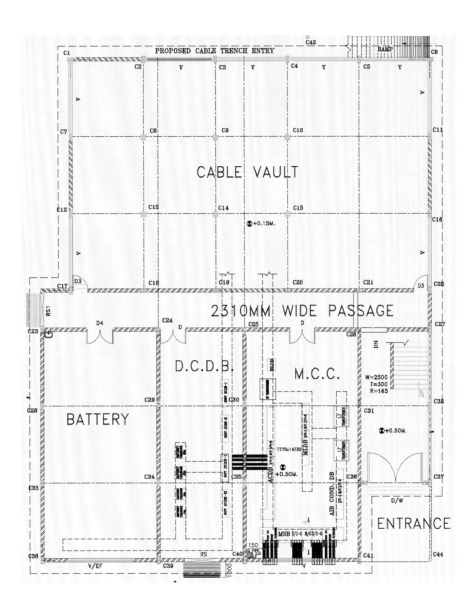

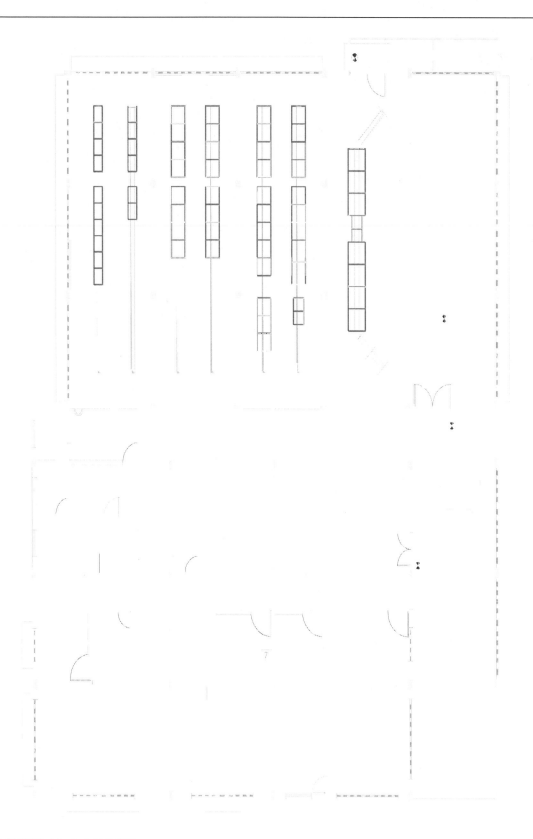

20. STRUCTURAL LAYOUT

21. CIVIL LAYOUT

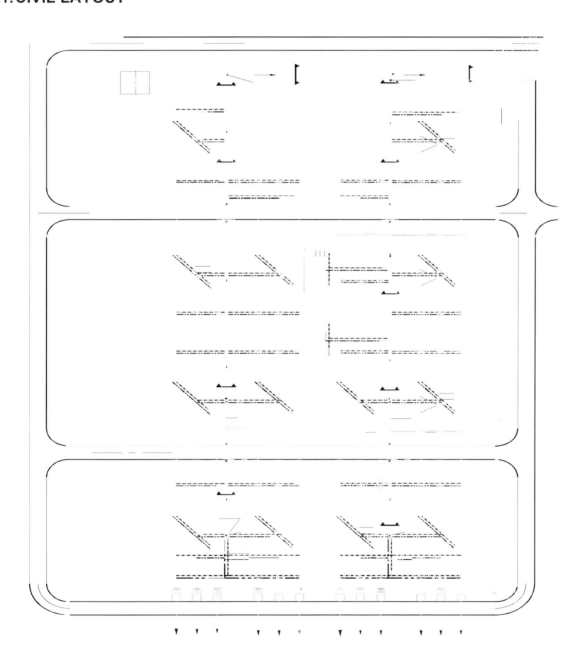

22. SUBSTATION LIGHTING DESIGN

- Adequate lighting is necessary for safety of working personnel and O&M activities

- Recommended value of Illumination level
    - Control & Relay panel area - 350 Lux (at floor level)
    - Test laboratory - 300 Lux
    - Battery room - 100 Lux
    - Other indoor area - 150 Lux
    - Switchyard - 50 Lux (main equipment)
      - 20 Lux (balance Area / road @ ground level)

23. SINGLE BUS ARRANGEMENT

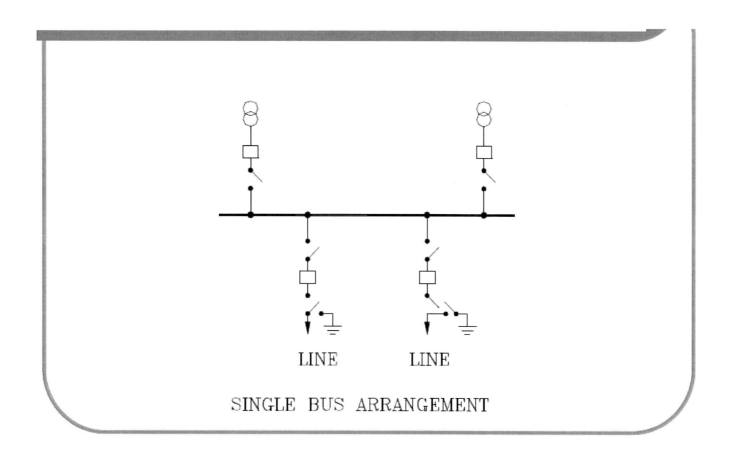

SINGLE BUS ARRANGEMENT

Merits	Demerits	Remarks
1. Low cost	1. Fault of bus or any circuit breaker results in shut-down of entire substation	1. Used for distribution substations upto 33kV
2. Simple to Operate	2. Difficult to do any maintenance	2. Not used for large substations.
3. Simple Protection	3. Bus cannot be extended without completely de-energizing substations	3. Sectionalizing increases flexibility
	4. Can be used only where loads can be interrupted or have other supply arrangements.	

24. MAIN & TRANSFER BUS ARRANGEMENT

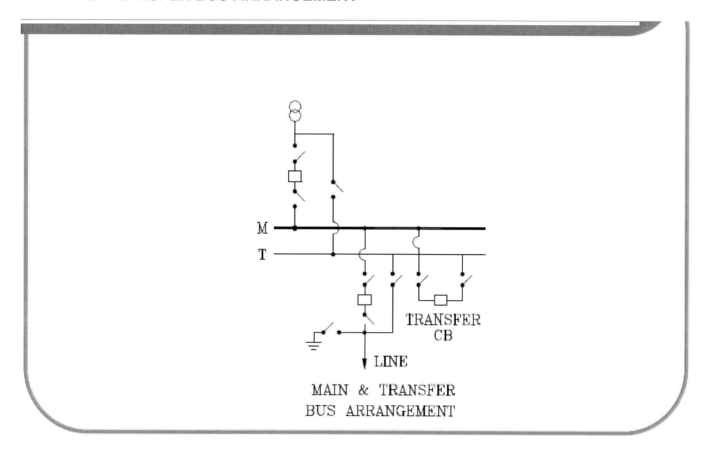

MAIN & TRANSFER
BUS ARRANGEMENT

Merits	Demerits	Remarks
1. Low initial & ultimate cost	1. Requires one extra breaker coupler	1. Used for 110kV substations where cost of duplicate bus bar system is not justified
2. Any breaker can be taken out of service for maintenance.	2. Switching is somewhat complex when maintaining a breaker	.
3. Potential devices may be used on the main bus	3. Fault of bus or any circuit breaker results in shutdown of entire substation.	

25. DOUBLE BUS WITH SINGLE BREAKER ARRANGEMENT

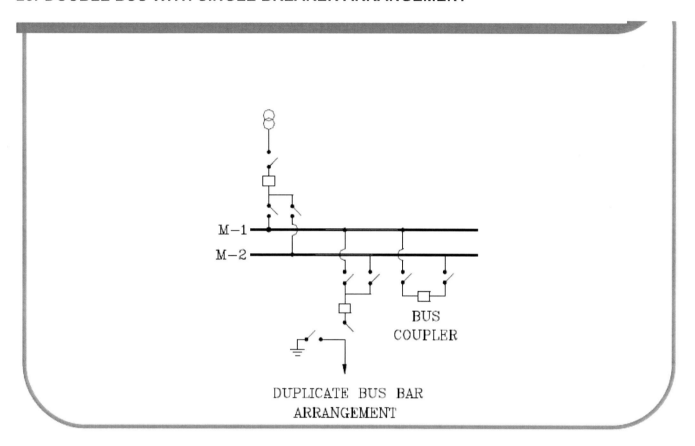

M-1

M-2

BUS
COUPLER

DUPLICATE BUS BAR
ARRANGEMENT

Merits	Demerits	Remarks
1. High flexibility 2. Half of the feeders connected to each bus	1. Extra bus-coupler circuit breaker necessary. 2. Bus protection scheme may cause loss of substation when it operates. 3. High exposure to bus fault. 4. Line breaker failure takes all circuits connected to the bus out of service. 5. Bus couplers failure takes entire substation out of service.	1. Most widely used for 66kV, 132kv, 220kV and important 11kv, 6.6kV, 3.3kV substations.

26. DOUBLE BUS WITH DOUBLE BREAKER ARRANGEMENT

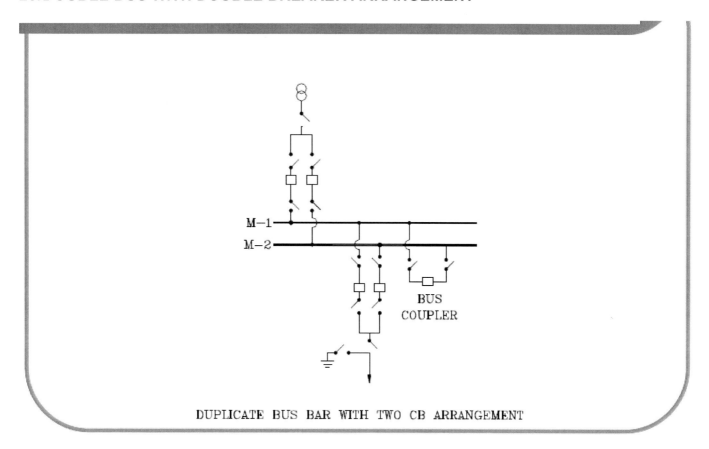

DUPLICATE BUS BAR WITH TWO CB ARRANGEMENT

Merits	Demerits	Remarks
1. Each has two associated breakers	1. Most expensive	1. Not used for usual EHV substations due to high cost.
2. Has flexibility in permitting feeder circuits to be connected to any bus	2. Would lose half of the circuits for breaker fault if circuits are not connected to both the buses.	2. Used only for very important, high power, EHV substations.
3. Any breaker can be taken out of service for maintenance.		
4. High reliability		

27. DOUBLE MAIN & TRANSFER

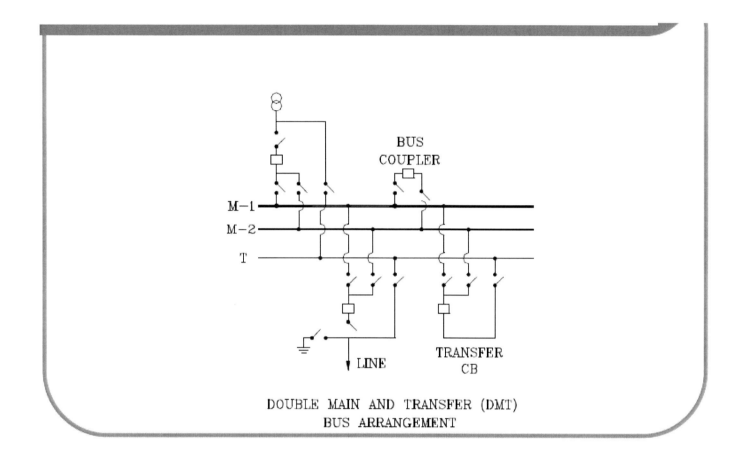

DOUBLE MAIN AND TRANSFER (DMT)
BUS ARRANGEMENT

Merits	Demerits	Remarks
1. Most flexible in operation	1. High cost due to three buses	1. Preferred by some utilities for 400kV and 220kV important substations.
2. Highly reliable		
3. Breaker failure on bus side breaker removes only one ckt. From service		
4. All switching done with breakers		
5. Simple operation, no isolator switching required		
6. Either main bus can be taken out of service at any time for maintenance.		
7. Bus fault does not remove any feeder from the service		

28. ONE & HALF BREAKER SCHEME

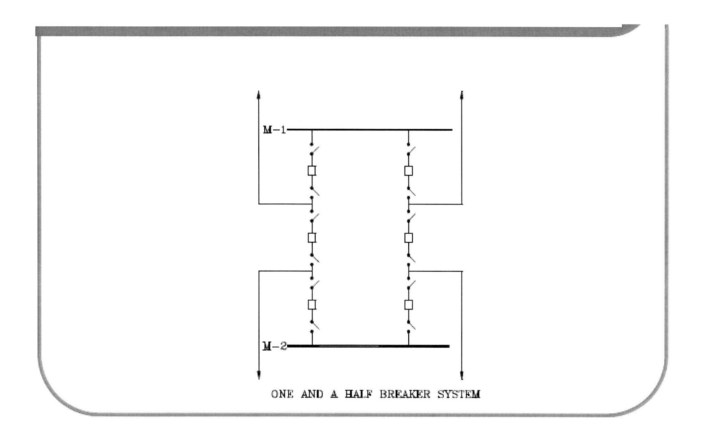

ONE AND A HALF BREAKER SYSTEM

Merits	Demerits	Remarks
1. Flexible operation for breaker maintenance	1. One and half breakers per circuit, hence higher cost	1. Used for 400kV & 220kV substations.
2. Any breaker can be removed from maintenance without interruption of load.	2. Protection and auto-reclosing more complex since middle breaker must be responsive to both associated circuits.	2. Preferred.
3. Requires 1 1/2 breaker per feeder.		
4. Each circuit fed by two breakers.		
5. All switching by breaker.		
6. Selective tripping		

29. RING BUS ARRANGEMENT

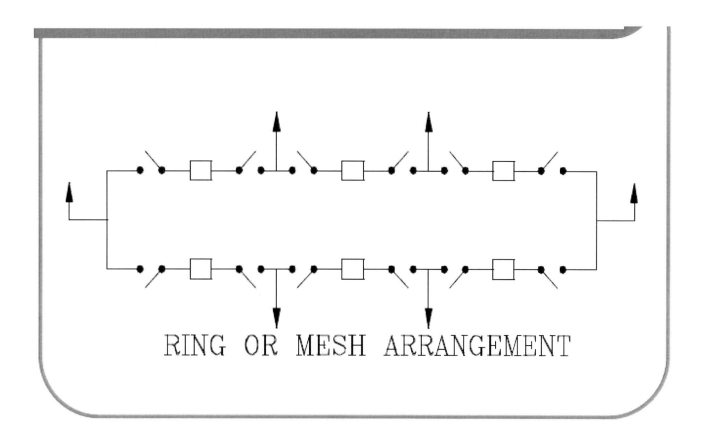

RING OR MESH ARRANGEMENT

Merits	Demerits	Remarks
1. Busbars gave some operational flexibility	1. If fault occurs during bus maintenance, ring gets separated into two sections. 2. Auto-reclosing and protection complex. 3. Requires VT's on all circuits because there is no definite voltage reference point. These VT's may be required in all cases for synchronizing live line or voltage indication 4. Breaker failure during fault on one circuit causes loss of additional circuit because of breaker failure.	1. Most widely used for very large power stations having large no. of incoming and outgoing lines and high power transfer.

30. MINIMUM CLEARANCES

BASIC DESIGN OF 400/220KV SUB-STATION

	400kV	220kV
1. Phase to Earth	3500 mm	2100 mm
2. Phase to phase	4200 mm (Rod-conductor configuration) 4000 mm (Conductor-conductor configuration)	2100 mm
3. Sectional clearance	6400 mm	4300 mm

BASIC DESIGN OF 400/220KV SUB-STATION

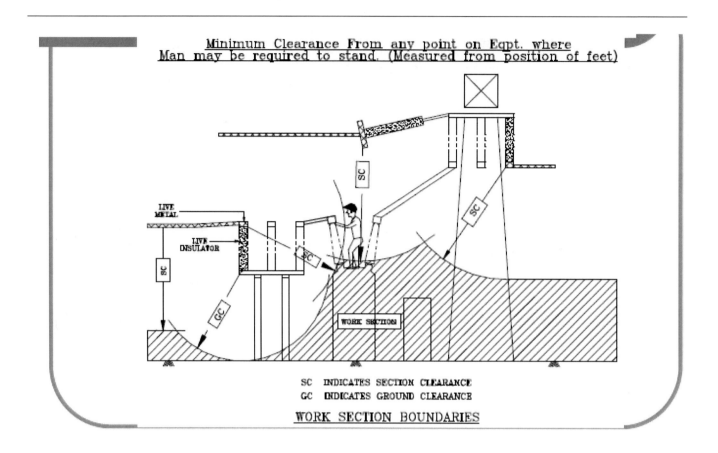

Minimum Clearance From any point on Eqpt. where
Man may be required to stand. (Measured from position of feet)

SC INDICATES SECTION CLEARANCE
GC INDICATES GROUND CLEARANCE

WORK SECTION BOUNDARIES

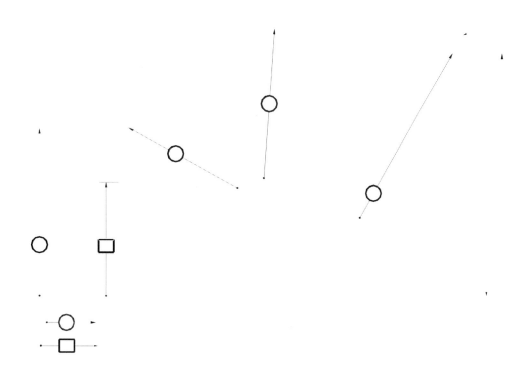

31. CLEARANCES DIAGRAM

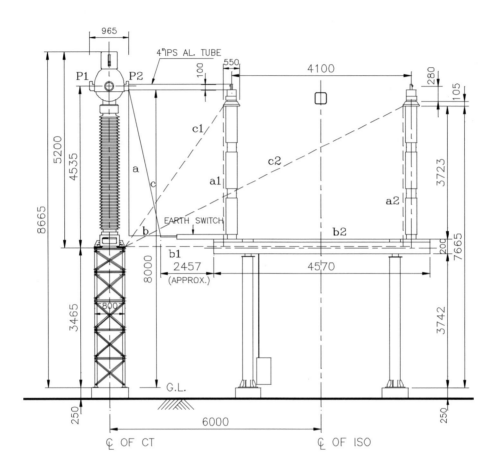

32. BUS BAR DESIGN

- Continuous current rating. Ampacity caculation as per IEEE:738

- Short time current rating (40kA for 1 Sec.) IEC-865

- Stresses in Tubular Busbar

- Natural frequency of Tubular Busbar

- Deflection of Tube

- Cantilever strength of Post Insulator

- Aeolian Vibrations

33. GANTRY STRUCTURE DESIGN

- **Sag / Tension calculation : as per IS: 802 1995**

Sr.	Temp	Wind Pressure	Limits
1.	Min.	No wind	
2.	Min.	36%	
3.	Every Day	No wind	T <= 22% of UTS
4.	Every Day	100%	T <= 70% of UTS
5.	Max. (ACSR 75^{0}C/ AAAC 85^{0}C)	No wind	Clearances

- **Short Circuit Forces calculation**
  As per IEC : 865
  Short circuit forces during short circuit
  Short circuit forces after short circuit
  Short circuit forces due to "Pinch" effect for Bundled conductor
  Spacer span calculation

- **Factor of safety of 2.0 under normal condition and 1.5 under short circuit condition**

34. SPACER SPAN VS SHORT CKT. FORCES

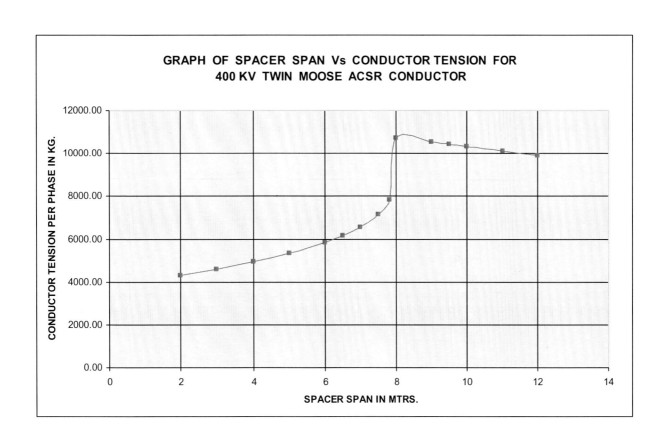

35. EARTHING DESIGN

- Guiding standards – IEEE 80, IS:3043, CBIP-223.
- 400kV & 220kV system are designed for 40kA.
- Basic Objectives:
  - Step potential ⎫ within tolerable
  - Touch Potential ⎬ limit
  - Ground Resistance
  - Adequacy of Ground conductor for fault current (considering corrosion)

Touch and step potential

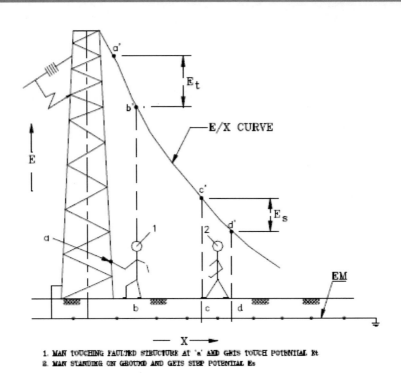

1. MAN TOUCHING FAULTED STRUCTURE AT 'a' AND GETS TOUCH POTENTIAL Et
2. MAN STANDING ON GROUND AND GETS STEP POTENTIAL Es

36. LIGHTNING PROTECTION-GROUND WIRE/LIGHTNING MAST

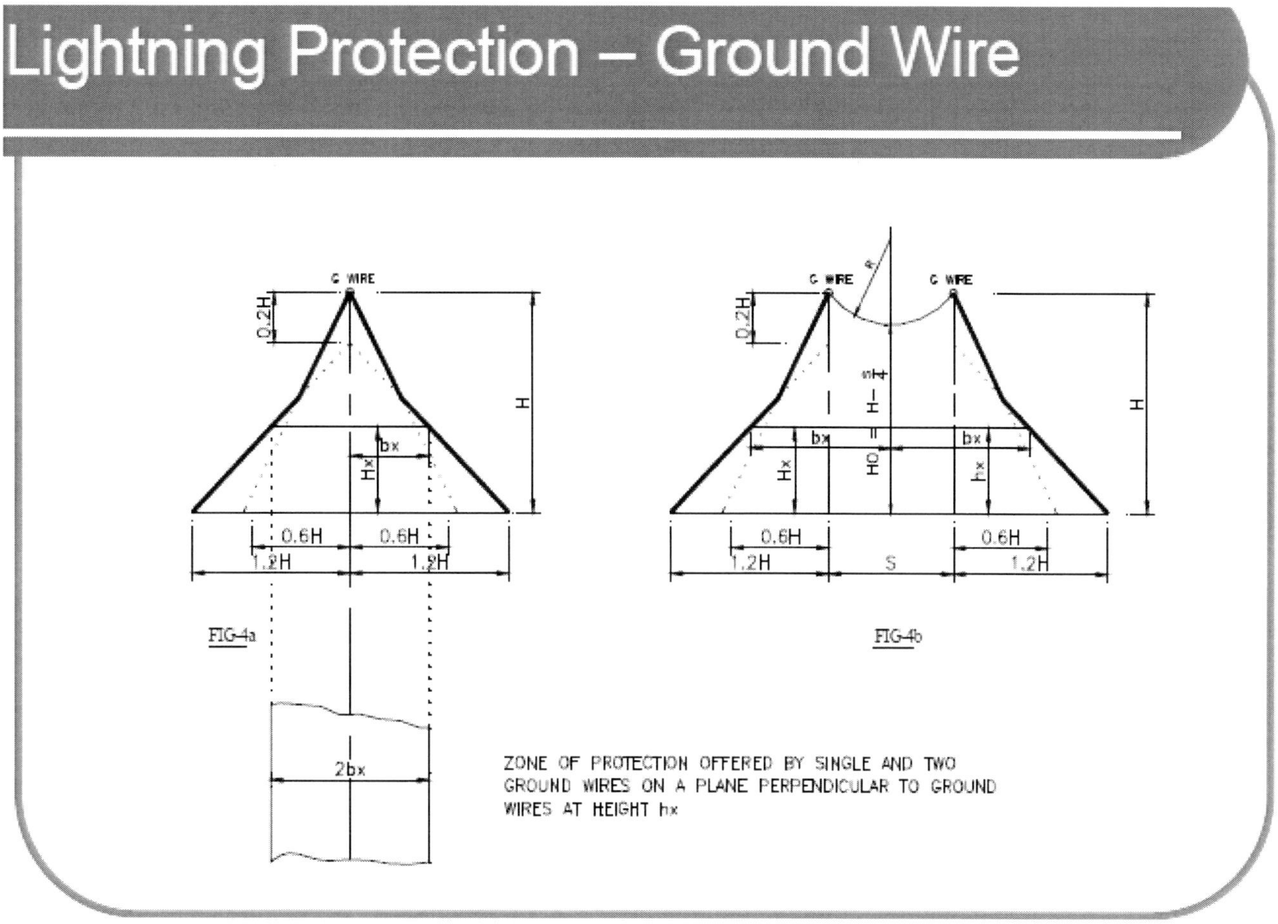

Lightning Protection – Ground Wire

FIG-4a

FIG-4b

ZONE OF PROTECTION OFFERED BY SINGLE AND TWO GROUND WIRES ON A PLANE PERPENDICULAR TO GROUND WIRES AT HEIGHT hx

Lightning Protection – Lightning Mast

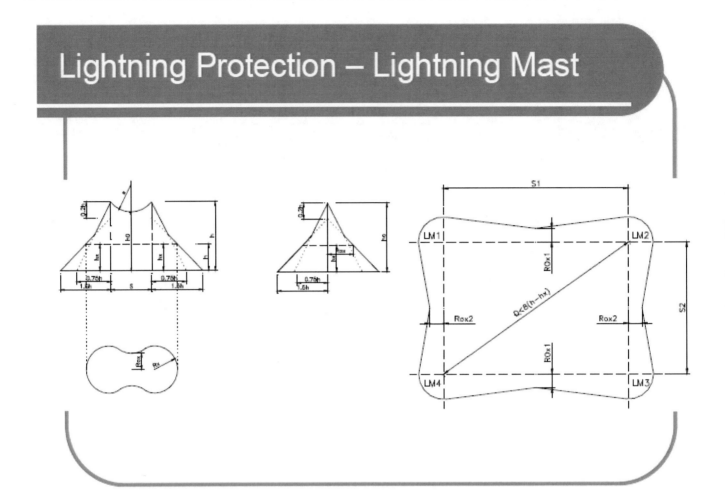